Congratulations Graduate!

William Nesmith

Thomas Nelson, Inc., Publishers
Nashville / New York / Camden

Library of Congress Cataloging in Publication Data

Nesmith, William, 1948-
    Congratulations, graduate!

    SUMMARY: Fourteen essays with advice to the graduate, using
material drawn from the American scene.
    1. Youth—Conduct of life.   [1. Conduct of life]
I. Title.
BJ1661.N38   170′.202′23   75-2346
ISBN-0-8407-4044-1

To
You, the new graduate
Upon your passing
One of life's
Significant
Milestones

Contents

Congratulations, Graduate!

ONE

Welcome
to the World!

*T*here are milestones in life. Graduation is one of them. It may be the most important. And you have just passed that milestone. Congratulations!

Somewhere, someday, some school or university or academy will erect a giant banner over the doors through which the members of a graduating class pass after being presented their diplomas; and the words on that banner will read:

"WELCOME TO THE WORLD!"

For that is what is implied when the diploma is in your hands, the milestone is behind you, and the next stage of the journey down the highway of life is before you.

To paraphrase an ancient proverb: "The journey of a thousand joys begins with a single anticipation." For no one welcomes a person to an unpleasant place. Welcomes are for the joyous, the happy, the hospitable

11

habitations of man. If you are being welcomed to the world, then it is a joyous occasion, a time of anticipation.

Ah, but . . .

There are those who say the world is not a very hospitable place. In fact, there are those who say it can be downright dangerous—that instead of life being a broad and comfortable highway into a pleasant city, it is a narrow and twisting path through a vicious jungle. Some would even say that the world is so bad, and its Creator so disgusted with it, that any welcome to the world is a fraud: that all the good times are gone; that only trouble lies ahead; that the end of it all is imminent.

Which view is correct?

Is the world to which you are welcomed more good than bad? Or more bad than good?

Well, now.

Does it really matter?

Does it make any difference if the road ahead is not completely smooth and safe? Isn't it yours? To cope with its problems? Transcend its troubles? Enjoy its triumphs and treasures?

Psychiatrists—those funny little nuts who tell us when we're nuts—point out that human beings almost always experience a moment of letdown after any great achievement. At any point in the history of the world—in any country—there are usually enough great achievements to produce the feeling in some persons that all is over with the world. Ironically, however, the next generation has usually produced even bigger achievements!

True, some times have been better than others. And some times have been worse.

What has mattered has not been whether times have been good or bad, but what specific individuals have done with their own times.

The outlook of this book is that you have been handed a great, wide, beautiful, wonderful, changing world—that it is exciting to be alive today! Congratulations! Welcome to a wonderful world!

No matter where you live.

If tomorrow you walk down the streets of New York City, you will find yourself a part of a crowd of some of the most dynamic and knowledgeable persons on earth. Those aloof and impassive stone lions that guard the Public Library, have they ever seen such people before?

Go west across this great continent. Portland, Oregon. The sleeping giant that is snow-clad Mount Hood towers over a green and lovely land.

Go east to Atlanta, Georgia. Would Sherman burn it today?

And anywhere in between.

The excitement in Washington, D.C., is enough to make the statue of Admiral Farragut come alive, step down from its stone pedestal, and ask, "What's going on here?"

The hustle and bustle of Houston, Texas, is enough to make you think that Sam Houston and William Travis were pikers for dreaming of what Texas might become—unless you get lost on the freeways.

13

In Los Angeles, California, where you will get lost on the freeways, the very air (when there is any) smells of a new spirit of America on the move.

Chicago. Saint Louis. Memphis. New Orleans. Miami. Denver. The big cities and the small towns. The North, the South, the East, the West.

And, particularly, your own home town.

Was there ever such a world before?

And it's all yours.

Congratulations, graduate.

Welcome to the world!

TWO

The Challenge
of the Future

The story of *Rip Van Winkle* is a "reverse parable" for our time. Washington Irving's hero, who fell asleep for twenty years, returned to a world that was very similar to the one he left. Aside from the fact that the people he had known had aged or died, nothing much had changed in his village.

Not today.

Our world is changing so rapidly that a modern day Rip Van Winkle, if he returned after twenty years, would probably think he was on another planet.

Ah, you ask, what's good about that? What does fast change mean to me?

Well, change, of course, is not something that happens by itself. Change is caused by persons. Men and women invent new machines. Men and women develop new technological processes. Persons change the face of their environment; the environment does not do it by itself.

At the beginning of the twentieth century, Henry Ford began the process that transformed the "horseless carriage" from a "rich man's toy" to the automobile that remade America. Working in a tiny brick building (the original is in Dearborn Village, Detroit, today; you and I would consider it too small to manufacture a barbecue grill), he produced his first successful "car." When he got ready to take it out for a test run, he had to knock bricks out of the doorway with a sledgehammer to get his contraption outside. His neighbors could not have known how those few sledgehammer blows were going to change the world their children would know.

True, it is doubtful if Henry Ford ever considered that he was responding to "the challenge of the future" when he built his first gasoline vehicle. He was simply being himself, doing what he did best, doing what he wanted to do.

(You know, of course, that in the early days he even *raced* his own cars. Personally. Did well at it, too. And that was long before the NASCAR you have known. Richard Petty, eat your heart out.)

But that may be the point of the whole thing.

The men and women who really meet "the challenge of the future" are not the ones who talk about it; they are the ones who do something about it. What they do is usually the thing they do best, the thing they want to do.

Not always, of course.

This same Henry Ford is often given credit for introducing mass production and the assembly line to

America. Well, yes—and no. Eli Whitney, the cotton gin man, needing interchangeable parts for the guns he built, is usually chosen by the historians as the father of mass production.

(No, Lucinda, it is not a typographical error. Friend Eli built guns as well as gins. Look it up in the history books.)

What apparently happened is that Henry Ford decided he was going to sell his Model T automobile for a certain fixed low price. He told his engineers to produce a car that could be sold at a profit at that price. The only way to do it was the assembly line, standardization—and certain other things that went along with it such as: "Give the customer any color car she wants as long as it is black."

But the automobile and the assembly line did change America. In less than three-quarters of a century the country went from a land of small towns and a few big cities, to industrial cities, to spreading suburbia—and your generation will probably take it back to rural life again (but that is another story).

The challenge of the future.

When Henry Ford's sledgehammer knocked the bricks out of his doorway that dark morning so long ago, the future probably seemed relatively tame. Today, when that future is the past, we know how much has been accomplished, how big the unseen challenge at the turn of the century was. Therefore, if the challenge of today's future sometimes seems *too* challenging—what with population problems, energy shortages, social restlessness, technological oppression, ecological nightmares, and sundry assorted ills—remember that you're big enough to handle the challenge.

Congratulations, graduate.

You got yourself a live one!

THREE

The Values
That Last

The place was Stockholm, Sweden. The occasion, the presentation of the Nobel Prize in Literature, our modern world's highest honor to a writer.

There was one unusual note.

This second half of the twentieth century is a time of tremendous change. The changes have come so fast that most older people have been so alarmed by them that they despair of the present and are frightened by the future. Once they would have said, "The world is going to the dogs." (Considering the price of dog food in the affluent American world past the mid-century, "going to the dogs" would have been a pretty expensive *gotterdammerung!*)

But the usual complaint now is that today's world has discarded all the old values. To the elders, the loss of the old values that made sense out of the world into which they were born is the most terrible thing about our times. To them such a loss automatically means that living in today's world is like roaring down the freeway at top speed in an automobile that has no steering gear.

Stop a minute.

Notice that no one has ever really *proved* that the "old values" have disappeared from the world. The assumption has simply been made that, since things aren't "the way they were"—whatever that was—things must be hopeless. For that matter, how many of the older generation that you know can even tell you what their "old values" were?

Er . . .

Of course . . .

It's a nasty question to ask, but . . .

What about you? Do you know what *your* values are?

So, let's go back to Stockholm, Sweden.

December 10, 1950.

The man, of course, was William Faulkner, American writer. He came from half a world away, Mississippi in the American South; yet here in the European North he looked oddly at home, a "distinguished" gray-haired gentleman. He made a very short speech of acceptance, and in that speech were some words you and I might want to ponder.

He spoke of mankind enduring and prevailing. And then, indirectly, he gave his own list of the old values:

Courage—

Honor—

Hope—

Pride—

Compassion—

Pity—

Sacrifice.

He called these abstract qualities of man "the glory of his past."

Think of them for a minute.

Courage. Honor. Hope. Pride. Compassion. Pity. Sacrifice.

It's a nice feeling to belong to the human race if courage, honor, hope, pride, compassion, pity, and sacrifice are the attributes of such a race, is it not?

In the long history of mankind, aren't these the values that have lasted best? Aren't these the qualities that we would want to prevail? In truth, are they not the appealing "old verities"?

No matter how much the world may change in the future, as long as persons are courageous, honorable, hopeful, proud of being human beings—as long as they show compassion and pity—as long as they retain the capacity to sacrifice for worthy ends, will not the world be a challenging and human place in which to live?

Welcome to that world. Welcome, graduate, to the old values.

And, just in case you have some misgivings in listening to the words of a mere writer, remember that Faulkner, mere writer though he may have been, was willing to put his words on the line. As a young man, before the entrance of the United States into the First World War, he had gone to Canada and enlisted in the Royal Canadian Air Force. In his own words: "I

21

had seen an aeroplane and my mind was filled with names: Ball, and Immelman and Boelcke, and Guynemer and Bishop . . ."

Faulkner's dreams may not have been what you and I might dream about. Even his list of the old verities may not be the list that you and I might compile.

But that there are values that last is undeniable. Do with your own what you will.

FOUR

One Person
Alone

It takes 22 men to play football." A perfectly obvious statement.

What's wrong with such a statement? (Yes, Junior, 22 *women* could play football—but that's not the issue here.)

The point is that there is nothing wrong with the statement. Football is the team game par excellence. But thereby hangs a tale.

Why is football, which is a team game, such a favorite in America, the country which prides itself on its individualism? Why not golf? Or tennis? On the face of it, it would seem that football ought to be the favorite of the Soviet Union and the other Communist countries who pride themselves on their collective societies. Instead, they go wild over soccer, which resembles a mob in search of a revolution. In contrast, football is regimented, disciplined, and orderly. And a team game.

So?

Think for a minute.

The ball is snapped. The quarterback has the ball. He fades back, looking for an eligible receiver.

At that one point in time he is the loneliest man in the stadium. There may be a hundred thousand persons in the stands. There may be millions watching on television. But for one frozen moment of time only one person counts: the man with the ball, the quarterback. It all depends on him. Does he pass? Does he run?

Play after play in any game, week after week during the season, city after city, one of the most intriguing paradoxes of civilized life is acted out upon the clipped grass or artificial turf—the paradox of the individual and the team.

Maybe you have never thought of it in such a way, but that paradox is one of the fundamental features of the world to which you have been welcomed. The world of mankind is a team world—but it depends upon individuals. It depends upon the man who has the ball.

More often than we are willing to admit, one man alone decides the destiny of many. The "big" events go down in the history books:

The late President Kennedy duelling with Soviet Premier Khrushchev over nuclear missiles in Cuba, atomic war that could destroy the world at stake—

Dogged, implacable Winston Churchill rallying England after Dunkirk—

Christopher Columbus sailing west—

Charles Martel at Tours and Poitiers in A.D. 732, stopping the Saracens.

But the "little" events are the ones that count for the most because they come to all of us. Day after day, life after life, there come the times when a person "has the ball." It may be a decision affecting only him or her, or his or her family. It may not even be a big decision. But it will be a time for that one person—and that one person alone—to act. The world before you is full of such moments, moments that call for courage and integrity—perhaps even sacrifice.

But let's not get carried away.

Remember the quarterback?

Sure, he has the ball. He's all alone. He's looking for an eligible receiver.

But he didn't do it all by himself, friend.

The line held. The blitz didn't get through and sack him before he had a chance to throw. The team was still there. For that matter, if he throws a pass, the success of his action will depend as much on what the receiver can do as on the throw itself. If he runs, he will have to count on the blocking he gets from his own team. So it cuts both ways. The individual and the team. The team and the individual. Both need each other.

Graduate, such is the world before you. When the times come for you to carry the ball, best wishes to you. We're cheering you on. You're that one person alone out there. Courage. Integrity. Skill. May they all be with you.

And, if the time comes when you feel that you are too much alone, that carrying the ball is more than you bargained for, this advice from the sidelines:

Remember the team. You don't always have to do it all by yourself.

Sometimes, yes.

But not always.

25

John Donne said that no man is an island unto himself, that we are all part of the continent. He was living on the "island" of England when he said it, however.

So—

Either way it works out—

Individual or team—

Congratulations!

FIVE

The Bright Horizon

*T*he trouble with advice that old people give is that it is always too high-flown. To take these people seriously, one would think that life is nothing but one crisis after another, that every decision is a life-or-death matter, that it's all a big deal. Haven't these people ever heard of blah days?

I was in Cleveland, Ohio. Now, Ohio is a very fine state. I like it. Cleveland is a large city. There are a lot of buildings and people and cars and such American things in Cleveland and the surrounding area. But this wasn't one of those big days; it was a blah day.

Ever had a blah day?

Graduate, whether you know it or not, the world to which you are welcomed is full of blah days. What do you do with them? Let me tell you about mine; maybe it will mean something to you.

I had an eight o'clock appointment in Cleveland. The man cancelled. So what? No big deal. Who wants to talk business at eight o'clock in the morning anyway?

I drove to Ravenna. Nice drive. Light traffic. The rental car was brand-new. The music on the radio was pleasant. But no big deal. Nothing to go ape over. A blah morning. But not unpleasant.

The man I was to see in Ravenna was late. I had to wait for him. His office building was on the outskirts of town, so I walked outside while I waited. It was an Ohio morning in the middle of Fall. Nothing fancy about it. Just morning. But the man's office building was next to farmland. I stood by the fence of the parking lot and looked at a horse a couple of hundred yards away in the pasture.

Now that was something to think about.

The company wasn't paying me to stand at a fence in Ohio and look at a horse. As far as I know, horse-looking not only is not in my job description, it is not in any job description in any major corporation in America. (I have no statistics for the People's Republic of China.)

A horse is a horse. I considered the possibility that I had seen the identical horse in Pennsylvania, outside Lancaster. But that didn't seem likely. Horses don't travel around the country very much. At least, I don't think they do. I may be wrong.

A pasture is a pasture. I was certain I had seen the same pasture outside Portland, Oregon. But that seemed even more unlikely. Pastures *don't* travel around the

28

country. I am certain. (Well, to be on the safe side, at least 99 44/100 percent certain . . .)

I thought about horse-watching.

(If I ever have to do any horse-watching in New York City, I am going to demand hazardous duty pay from the company. I probably won't get it.)

See what I mean?

A blah day.

I went back in the man's office and talked to him. A competitor's representative had already gotten to him. Score: zero. Blah day.

I drove to Akron. The client's secretary was nice (*not* a blah fact!). The client was nice. But thunder and lightning did not attend our deliberations.

There were no horses to watch in Akron.

The drive back to Cleveland where I had an airplane to catch would be a nice comfortable one with a safe margin of time on my side.

I thought.

They work on Interstates, you know. They tear them up and erect "Detour" signs that don't always communicate the true facts of the situation.

Have you ever gotten lost in a strange suburb?

Without a map?

You know the scenario.

No one ever *stays* lost in an American suburb (though I have a vague memory of getting behind a forty-year-old Ford with a bumper sticker that read, "Remember Pearl Harbor," and a white-haired old geezer peering out the windshield on the driver's side . . .). I finally got back to the airport. I made it to the Hertz check-in at just about the time my watch told me my flight was to depart.

I had no chance of making it, but, you know, you try a little harder on a blah day. Sometimes luck is with you. Sometimes planes are delayed.

The flight attendant was getting ready to close the door of the 727. But fortune and flight attendants always smile on last-minute runners. I made it.

At this point it almost ceased being a blah day. Ever stumble into an airplane cabin at the very, very last minute? All those silent people strapped in their seats look at you as though you were an uninvited Martian who just crashed an exclusive wake.

There were no horses on the airplane.

But there was a very pretty stewardess.

And that's another story, graduate.

At forty thousand feet the horizon was very bright . . .

SIX

Goal
to Go!

C anada probably does not come to your mind when you watch a football game.

But, in my case . . .

Well, there is a special situation, and there are special circumstances.

The score is tied. There is a minute or less to play. The team you are rooting for has gotten the ball inside the ten-yard line. It's first down and goal to go. That's when I think of Canada.

Christmas vacation. I had met a person from Canada, and I was driving up to spend the holidays at her parents' home. I got caught in a Canadian snowstorm.

Canadian snowstorms are probably no different than United States snowstorms. This one just seemed to be. Or, maybe I and my Chevrolet were just so accustomed to the warmer climes of the middle of the United States that the storm seemed worse than it was. For awhile

I didn't worry. I had good directions. After all, both of us were graduate students when she gave me the directions. And don't graduate students know everything there is to know?

But the trip took longer and longer. The time got later and later. The afternoon got darker and darker. Then it was night, and I still was not there.

Finally, though, I came to the last fork in the road and turned off, I thought, from the provincial highway I had been following on to the county road that was to take me to my destination.

I followed the road the distance on my speedometer I had been told and came to the fanciest entrance to a farm I had ever seen. Not only was there a broad turnoff, there was a big stone wall, a huge iron gate, and a guard in a guardhouse.

The thought boggled my mind: Had I met some Canadian millionaire's daughter who lived on some baronial estate that covered half the province?

No.

The guard at the gate set me right.

Last turn, goal to go; but I had not taken the county road. I was still on the provincial highway. This was not her farmhouse. This was the provincial prison.

So now, when it's first down and goal to go, and the game is almost over, I want to yell to the quarterback: "Look out! You don't have it made. You still have to make the *right* play."

Because, you see, the final moments of any contest—in football, in business, in any life situation—are the critical moments. When it's "goal to go," you have to be right.

You have used up most of your margin for error. You're down to the wire. It's up to you.

In salesmanship, the most critical moments are those when "the sale is closed." Sales managers despair of the salesman who can do beautifully up to that point, then fail.

In war, it is the final battle that decides. In 1781, when Washington, Lafayette, von Steuben, Rochambeau, and de Grasse had Cornwallis cornered at Yorktown, it was all over; the American Revolution was won. On the other hand, during the Civil War, Lincoln pinned his hopes on general after general—including the otherwise remarkable McClellan—in vain until he found that Ulysses Simpson Grant could deliver when it was "goal to go."

In the arts, it is the final chapter of the book, the last scene in the play, the last forty feet of the film that wraps it all up.

And in human relationships, the same thing applies. Frontier America had a favorite expression: "You'll do to ride the river with." The meaning was that here was a friend who could be counted upon all the way—to the last.

Oddly enough, in one way or the other, most things in life are often closer to "goal to go" than we think. The situation doesn't always have to be desperate. In fact, the more times we "close the sale" while the situation is still under our control, the more successful we are likely to be.

Maybe what I am saying is that the world to which you are welcomed has many of the elements of a game—and you play to win, not lose. And you can win, even when all seems to be lost. The point was dramatically made in what has been called "the most exciting football game ever televised," the Conference decision contest between the Oakland Raiders and the Miami Dolphins late in 1974 when Ken Stabler, Oakland quarterback, threw the one final desperate, impossible pass that won the game.

So, when it's "goal to go" for you, here's good luck and best wishes.

By the way, I did find the farmhouse for which I was looking.

And Canada is a fine country.

I like it.

SEVEN

When Teamwork Counts

I have an acquaintance who has a thing about catalogs. He not only collects them, he hoards them. I have a sneaking suspicion he would probably even send off for a catalog of "Interior Appointments for Eskimo Igloos."

Of course, not all his catalogs are exotic.

The last time I saw him he had just received a new catalog from a small firm in Vermont. It was not a big catalog. But I was struck by something special, a distinctive in this catalog that has a lot of bearing on the kind of world into which you are welcomed.

Have you ever seen a catalog with "integrity"? Well, this one had integrity—spelled, "YANKEE."

That's right, "Yankee."

Whoever had written the copy knew his New England. He had to be a native Yankee himself to know that when he said, "sturdily made by Yankee craftsmen," he was describing the best workmanship, that this article came from a region stubbornly proud for generations of being "Yankee."

Seems as though, when you use the word "Yankee" in connection with a product, you are describing something honestly made and honestly represented.

Seems as though.

For the Yankee reputation is that of a man of few words, none of them unnecessary. It is the reputation for plainness, simplicity, sturdiness, self-reliance, and honesty.

Yankee is a proud word as Yankees use it—a synonym for integrity.

So what has this to do with teamwork and you?

Well, the world to which you are welcomed—particularly America—is made up of other groups than Yankees. Working together—in teamwork—they have built the greatest nation the world has ever seen.

(You know, of course, that even the *pessimistic* experts say that America will stay the world's greatest industrial nation almost to the end of the twentieth century—even under the *worst* conditions.)

America is not all Yankee.

There are the Southerners. They lost the decision at Appomattox Courthouse, but . . .

There are the Westerners. They haven't spent all their time sitting on a rock waiting to tell the posse: "They went that-a-way." Been to Houston lately? Or Dallas? Or Oke City?

The Californians.

The courageous men and women who tamed Utah.

The competent settlers of Wyoming.

Did you know that there are probably more people of Polish descent in the "crescent" south of the Great Lakes than there are in the entire nation of Poland? (And Poles have done more than invent the best-tasting sausage you will ever eat!)

The so-called "minorities." (The only thing minor about minorities is numerical; the accomplishments of American minorities are major.)

And that is only the beginning of the list. Ask yourself who you are and where you fit in. Ask who your neighbors are.

In short, there are a lot of us in this country, and each of us is a little bit different. Working together—in teamwork—our forefathers, who were *more* different than we, made this a great nation.

So . . .

The future looks bright.

But there is a catch.

All those groups that have made America, all those groups who have worked in teamwork to produce this amazing land, have been made up of single individuals like you and me. Teamwork is fine. It produces miracles. But it produces those miracles as the result of a lot of individual miracles wrought by individual persons.

When does teamwork count?

It counts all the time. It counts all the way. It counts on the job. It counts in the office. It counts in the home. It counts in the family.

If and when you get to the rarefied atmosphere of the rosewood-panelled executive suite—surprise! You'll find that teamwork counts in the corporation staff.

If—and this is unlikely—you find yourself on a Colorado sheep ranch—surprise! In all the snow and ewes, there is teamwork between sheepherder and dogs.

There is something very nice about teamwork. There is a sense of satisfaction in being part of a group building something of value together.

You might even say that this is one of the added benefits of being in the world to which you are welcomed.

Congratulations!

Welcome to the team.

EIGHT

Try
a Little Harder

What do California redwoods have in common with Georgia cobblestones?

The General Sherman sequoia tree in Sequoia National Park is 3,500 or so years old. It stands 272 feet high. It is an awe-inspiring thing to see. It would be awe-inspiring all by itself, but Sequoia National Park contains groves of the giant trees. They are the largest and probably the oldest living things on this planet.

(In the same park is also Mount Whitney, which just happens to be the tallest mountain in the lower 48 states of the Union.)

You could say, after a visit to Sequoia National Park, that here Nature has tried a little harder—and made it.

If you are a Californian, you know that there are actually two species of sequoia trees. The General Sherman tree and those like it are *Sequoia gigantea.* A different species is *Sequoia sempervirens,* source of the redwood

39

lumber that grows in a narrow strip of coast mountain ranges from the southern part of Oregon to the Bay of Monterey. This smaller tree is alwo awe-inspiring. There is a state park not far from San Jose that will give you the full effect. You will have been driving through ordinary California mountain countryside; you come into the entrance and park; you get out and walk among the trees; and suddenly you are in another world: it is as though you are in some vast natural cathedral, hushed since the Creation. It is hard to imagine that another sequoia species has tried a little harder; this one seems to have done all that can be done!

But the cobblestones of Georgia . . .

Savannah, Georgia, is an old, old city. Not 3,500 years old, of course. (But, oddly, an old Savannah building *seems* older than a California redwood . . .) The sense of history is strong. If you live in Savannah, you show visitors the old buildings, particularly the old churches, since John Wesley lived here for a spell and had an unfortunate love affair—and the idea of the kind of religious figure John Wesley was having an unfortunate love affair is guaranteed to boggle the mind.

Eventually you take the visitor down to the waterfront. This is where the cobblestones come in. In the early days, cobblestones were used to pave the streets. Cobblestones in Savannah are big, rounded rocks that came over to this country as ballast in ships. Cobblestones are probably satisfactory for horses (I haven't asked a horse about it), but try riding on a cobblestone road in a Volkswagen; you'll understand why most cobblestone streets have been blacktopped. There is a short section of street in Savannah going down to the river that is in its natural state—you bounce over the cobblestones.

As you bounce, you see the ships that have come in from the sea. For more than two centuries ships have come to Savannah. Though it is 18 miles from the Atlantic Ocean, it has an excellent landlocked harbor, open the year around. Savannah is an important seaport. In fact, the first steamship to cross the Atlantic, the *Savannah*, in 1819, was Savannah-owned and started her voyage from Savannah. The first commercial nuclear ship built by America was also named *Savannah*.

So, if you are imaginative, with your feet upon the cobblestones and your eyes upon the foreign shipping in the river, you think.

What if nothing in the world had been changed since 1733 when General James Oglethorpe founded Savannah?

The cobblestones under your feet give you one idea of what that world might be.

But that is not the way the world is. High in the Georgia sky an airliner moves against the blue of space. Here closer at hand, on the river, a freighter from Holland carries the commerce of Europe and America.

What made the difference?

Well, somebody tried a little harder.

The man who designed the steamship *Savannah* was trying a little harder than his colleagues who were designing sailing ships at the time. The world of jets and automobiles and atoms, the world of technology, has come into being because men have tried a little harder.

41

And, in individual life after individual life, the man who has succeeded has been the man who has tried a little harder.

So, graduate, congratulations on being in that kind of world, a world where, if you try a little harder, you'll make it.

Just don't try to outlive a sequoia tree.

There's Always
a Second Chance

*I*f you think you have troubles, consider the case of a farm boy born in Pleasant, Ohio, in 1822, Hiram Ulysses Grant. If ever there was proof of the adage, "there's always a second chance," his life is it. There is a catch, of course; he happened to be a person of remarkable courage and determination. He came back on the second chance not once, but many times.

Hiram Grant wasn't much of a farmer. He decided to go to West Point and become an army officer. The Congressman who got him his appointment goofed (times haven't changed much, have they?), and got him the appointment under the wrong name, Ulysses Simpson Grant. Grant changed his name to that.

Grant was not the best student who had ever attended West Point. Maybe one of the laziest. Certainly one of the sloppiest dressers. But after his graduation he got a second chance; in the Mexican War he did a great job and was promoted to first lieutenant.

After the war, the story was different. Assigned to service in the American West, Grant drank too much and was ordered by his commanding general to shape up or ship out. He shipped out.

He tried farming and failed. He tried being a real estate agent and failed. He tried working for the United States Customhouse and failed. He tried working in his father's hardware store in Galena, Illinois, and failed again.

A thirty-eight-year-old who couldn't even make it in his papa's store.

Hmn . . .

When the Civil War broke out, Grant went back to soldiering. It is not recorded that there was excessive joy in the War Department over his decision. In fact, there is some evidence to the contrary: his request for a colonelcy was ignored; he had to get the appointment from the governor of Illinois.

Grant was 40 years old, with a very poor track record. However . . .

There's always a second chance.

Many times over in Grant's case.

By August of 1861 he had been promoted brigadier general of volunteers. As commander of the forces in southwestern Missouri he embarked upon a career of victory after victory. The first major Union victory was his, the capture of Forts Henry and Donelson. Because of the terms of surrender he imposed in this case, the

"U. S." in his name was hailed as a nickname, "Unconditional Surrender Grant."

He went up the ladder, winning victory after victory. Shiloh, Vicksburg, and Chattanooga are the ones you read about in the history books.

Finally, in March, 1864, President Lincoln made him a lieutenant-general, put him in command of all the Union armies with responsibility to no one but the President, and Grant took on the "big one"—General Robert E. Lee, brilliant commander of the Confederate forces.

Grant won.

Appomattox.

The end.

(And yet, he was a pretty decent fellow in victory. His terms to Lee were generous. Men of integrity usually are generous in victory.)

In 1866 he received an honor that heretofore had been reserved only for George Washington; he was made a full general.

He had it made.

One would have thought that he had used up his string of second chances, that they would never be needed again in his case.

He was elected President.

Now, that was a mistake.

Ulysses Simpson Grant had been an extremely successful general. He was not an extremely successful President. He had to contend with all kinds of problems. Scandal racked his second administration. Honest himself, he did not understand some of the seamier facts of politics.

After the Presidency, he was cheated out of his fortune by a fraudulent banking firm. He was stricken with cancer.

He had one last second chance left.

With death facing him, in pain, he completed his memoirs, and they were published by Mark Twain. They paid off his debts, provided for his family, and he died in peace.

Were his second chances mere random chance—or did his courage have something to do with them?

You decide.

The point of it all involves this one thing:

There's always a second chance.

Your welcome to this world carries that guarantee.

TEN

In the Footsteps
of Heroes

The snow had fallen all night, fine, clean, thick. The world was white and fresh, and the day was new.

Michael was three. He had a new pair of boots, and he was following his daddy to the car. He was trying to walk in his daddy's footsteps, stretching his three-year-old legs out to the limit, and he wasn't having a very easy time of it—but he was having a happy time. Every successful leap forward brought a shout of joy.

I thought back a number of years to a place a thousand miles away, to the white sands of Pensacola Beach on a brilliant April afternoon. I had been seven or so, and I, too, had walked in my father's footsteps. In imagination I could still feel the warm wet sand under my bare toes.

There is a trite old expression blamed on some anonymous Indian of long ago to the effect that the only way to understand another person is to walk in his moccasins. (Considering the things they get blamed with, no wonder Indians are so hard to get along with. What would one Indian be doing walking in another Indian's moccasins anyway? What's the matter with his own moccasins? And how did he get his hands on the other Indian's moccasins in the first place? What kind of Indian would let another Indian—Oh, well . . .)

But the truth of the matter is that we don't walk in another's footsteps for the purpose of understanding that person. We do so out of respect and admiration; and, in the case of fathers and daddies, out of love.

So, graduate, you ask what this has to do with you and the world to which you are welcomed.

Have you ever walked down Duke of Gloucester Street in restored Williamsburg, Virginia?

If you do, you'll feel that you are back at the beginning of America, that you are walking in the footsteps of the men and women who set this dream in motion.

Unlike many of the famous historical spots in America, there is this about Williamsburg: You are not overwhelmed by the memory of some one individual great man. Instead, you get the impression that it took more than Washington and Franklin to make the American dream come true; it took lesser heroes, too, and ordinary men and women with ordinary hopes and aspirations. Persons like you and me.

Oh, sure, there was Patrick Henry. But . . .

When you walk in the footsteps of heroes, you walk in the footsteps of very human human beings. Our forefathers weren't always right. For that matter, *their*

48

heroes were not always the ones you read about in the history books today. For instance, a "hero" blew into town here in the spring of 1776 (if you can call the ways of travelling to Williamsburg in 1776 "blowing"). He was the general named by the Continental Congress in March, 1776, to head the newly created Southern Department. He was the general the Congress considered second only to Washington as competent to command, Charles Lee. The Congress was wrong. Lee thought the British would not invade South Carolina but would strike at Virginia. He was wrong. There were some other things about Lee. He did not make it to permanent hero status.

Likewise, not all of the heroes in whose footsteps you may walk today will be your heroes all your life. There is a very good chance that you may become a greater hero yourself than many of those you look up to today. That's the kind of world to which you are welcomed. Congratulations. It's an open-ended world.

But three-year-old Michael in the snow doesn't think about things like that. He thinks only of his daddy. His daddy is the biggest hero in the world, the greatest man living. Michael's world is a very human world—and neither Michael nor you would want it any other way. The snow may be cold underfoot, but Michael's world is a warm and friendly world.

I look at Michael, and I wonder what he will think about when he is your age or mine. I wonder who his heroes will include then.

For, you see, when you walk in the footsteps of heroes, you walk in a path that leads somewhere. Heroes go

49

places—figuratively or literally. The heroes of our country have taken America a long way from Duke of Gloucester Street in Williamsburg, Virginia. But you may take it even farther—or in a different direction.

I salute you on the journey.

Good luck!

ELEVEN

On Judging
Strangers

*M*y friend, not everything in the world to which you are welcomed is as predictable and uniform as a computer printout sheet. Appearances can be deceiving. Not everything is as it seems. Even United States Presidents can be oddballs—or look like oddballs.

Take Zachary Taylor, for instance.

A more unPresident-looking President probably never rode into Washington. He did *not* look the part; if Madison Avenue had existed in his day, the imagemaker assigned to "sell" him would have given up in despair and gone back to Peoria.

Taylor had the head of a giant—but *not* the body to match. He was short, dumpy, and thick-necked. His legs were so short that he couldn't get on a horse by himself; he had to be helped aboard—and riding horses was a big deal in Taylor's day. It was essential in Taylor's pre-President occupation; Taylor was the first Regular Army general to become President. (Five Presidents before him had gone to war, but they were citizen soldiers, not Regular Army.)

However, it is not recorded that military purists were overjoyed at having the military ideal represented by Taylor; he was no "spit-and-polish" soldier. (Well, the spit part, maybe . . . Taylor chewed tobacco to excess; and he who chews . . .) He started out as the most unmilitary-looking officer in the Army; the higher he rose in rank, the worse he looked. For instance, he would ride into battle wearing a long linen duster flapping about him and an old battered straw hat jammed down on his head. Thereby hangs a tale, and the point of considering Zachary Taylor.

One day a hotshot second lieutenant fresh out of the immaculate environs of West Point saw this seedy-look-ing old "civilian" moseying along on a non-military-looking horse (the General's favorite, "Old Whitey"), rode up to him and said, "Say, old codger . . ." (Try that on a modern general and see what it gets you.) When he found out he was talking to the top honcho, he fell over his own polished boots apologizing. Taylor cut him short and came up with the one memorable statement by which he probably should be remembered: "Never judge a stranger by his clothes."

Never judge a stranger by his clothes. Well, Taylor would think that way, wouldn't he? He was prejudiced.

But . . .

How did he get to be President?

The events were as oddball as his appearance. Taylor had very little schooling. He was not a lawyer and knew no law. He was virtually innocent of the major "facts" of government. He not only didn't know anything about politics, he had never even voted in his life when he was nominated for President in 1848. Nobody knew how he stood on any of the great issues of the day, and it was probably a good thing that nobody asked him.

But behind that rough, crude exterior he was a pretty decent human being, a kindly man, a person of integrity. He had been a success as an Army general; his troops adored him and called him, affectionately, "Old Rough and Ready." Had he lived—he died after sixteen months in the White House—he might have changed the course of American history. There is a clue in one action that he took. One of the reasons for nominating him had been that he was a Southerner and could get Southern votes. But, as President, he faced a situation where some of his fellow-Southerners threatened to secede from the Union (they were a dozen years ahead of history). No! he thundered. Try seceding and he would lead the Army against them in person and hang them as traitors. They didn't. Integrity does communicate. They were quite certain he would.

Never judge a stranger by his clothes.

It doesn't have to be a person.

New ideas can come dressed in strange clothes.

Not everything in the world to which you are welcomed is uniform and predictable.

And that makes for a very interesting world.

Congratulations on being a part of it.

TWELVE

Changing Times

The times, they have a-changed. Or maybe you didn't read the Sports Section of the daily newspaper today.

In 1828, in Philadelphia (Pennsylvania, that is; in 1828 it would have been taken for granted for then Philadelphia was one of the major cities of the world), twenty-five young "gentlemen" formed the United Bowmen of Philadelphia, one of the beginnings of organized sports in America.

Mr. Adams was President of the country—John Quincy Adams, that is. It is something to boggle the mind to consider that archery should be one of the first of the organized sports in the United States. Our forefathers got their kicks out of a little horse racing, soccer, town ball (ancestor of Abner Doubleday's baseball), cock-fighting, and illegal bare-knuckle boxing; but none of these was really organized.

So, archery . . .

They had a uniform, these "young gentlemen." It was enough to boggle the mind, too. Oversized light pants. Undersized long-sleeved dark tunics that looked like a rip-off from war surplus West Point cadet tunics that had been through a shrink-em laundry. And hats. Man, what hats! They looked like a visored military cap (that hadn't grown up to adulthood!) topped by a super-giant pizza tin. And tiny pointed shoes that looked like dancing slippers from the Roaring Twenties.

Ah, what class! (Mean Joe Green, Hank Aaron, Gary Player, Catfish Hunter, Billie Jean King—don't bother to eat your hearts out . . .) When they bent their bows on the sward and let fly their winged missiles . . . well, you take it from there.

But it was a beginning. Times have changed.

That was the year that Mr. Noah Webster published his first dictionary. An old print shows him sitting in a fancy chair looking as smug as though he had just spelled correctly "serendipitously" (but that word didn't come into existence until the twentieth century).

Of course, times were a-changing even then. The first (*horse-drawn!*) railway was built only two years before, in 1826, at Quincy, Massachusetts. It was used to transport stone from a quarry. And some bright boy had learned that the "black stone" a few blacksmiths burned in their forges could be used for heating; so coal had begun to be mined.

There were no Polaroid cameras. The big deal was having your silhouette cut. You sat in a chair, and a strong light threw your shadow, which was cut out of black paper. (John Quincy Adams lived long enough to be photographed by the newfangled "daguerreotype process" in 1847, when he was 79.)

The times they have a-changed. So two additional congratulations to you are in order.

First, congratulations because you did not graduate in 1828. I don't think you would have liked that world. (Unless, of course, you're some kind of nut. But, if you're some kind of nut, there's no point in congratulating you anyway.)

Second, because times not only have changed, they probably will keep on changing.

And times that change are always ultimately friendly to persons who are young. (You are young, right? You didn't spend forty years in the first grade, did you? If you did, the task of congratulating you is outside the parameters of my ability.)

What do you do with the changes? How do you contribute to change? Well, no one can really be specific about you and change—unless it is you. But there are a few basic principles that have usually applied during the long history of man on this planet. One is that change is an opportunity to do things better than they have been done before. An opportunity, of course, not a certainty. Persons can goof, and often do. Things can be made worse by change. Another principle is that he who faces change using the advantages that he has usually does the best job. That is, doing the thing you do best gives you the best chance.

Maybe it all comes back to the matter of integrity. The Yankee quality of sturdy honesty. The quality of

being for real. The fake and the shoddy are usually un-
masked in the world to which you are welcomed; more
often than not, the quality endures.

And that makes for a good world.

Welcome to it!

THIRTEEN

When the Game Is Won

General Motors Institute advertising, run in several youth publications, featured Susan Nemeth, youngest assistant engineering professor at the Institute. Most of the ad showed this person skydiving, the very interesting hobby where one jumps out of an airplane and falls for awhile before pulling the ripcord on the parachute. While the ad was careful to point out that not all of the Institute's professors were female adventurers, it did emphasize that high competence in a conventional field could be coupled with high adventure in one's off-the-job life.

And, why not?

Most advice we get that is inspirational deals with the struggle to win. Get in the game. Try hard. Go for the goal. Win.

But what happens after the game is won?

(This is not to imply that the General Motors person has won so much that this is all she will ever do. If you have ever stood at the open door of an airplane and looked at that brown and green earth so far below you, you will forever stand in awe of skydivers. A person like that will probably keep on doing awesome things in this life . . .)

Here is where this ad hints at something.

Winning is fulfilment and accomplishment. You've done what you set out to do. So, logically, one of the first things that a person should feel when the game is won is a deep sense of satisfaction. There is an odd thing about a sense of satisfaction. It has a curious "expanding" action; when you have succeeded at being good at something, you feel bigger, able to take on more, able to reach out. There is an old cliche that says, if you want something done, ask a *busy* person to do it; it's just another way of approaching the same truth—if you do one thing well, you can usually do many things well.

Maybe this is an aspect of winning that is not played up enough. Down deep in our hearts, whether we admit it or not, each of us wants to grow as a person. It is part of the mysterious makeup of being human. If winning makes us grow, if winning widens our horizons—aren't these better reasons for winning than the usual mumbo-jumbo about our "aggressive instincts"?

Still not convinced?

Well, there is another way of looking at what you do when the game is won, a more conventional way. Early in 1975, when the Pittsburgh Steelers won Superbowl IX, there was a heartwarming side to the victory. The 72-year-old owner of that football team had his first Superbowl victory. He had bought the franchise 42 years before (for $2,500—and thereby hangs a tale of changing times!), but he had never had a comparable victory. Now he had.

One of the cliches is that victory is sweet. It was certainly sweet for the Steelers. But there was something else. Even before the stadium was emptied of its crowd, even before the television time was over, the sports experts were talking about the *future* of the team. The commentators pointed out that it was essentially a "young" team, that it had been built up from the draft rather than by trading. Consequently its best seasons should lie in the future.

See what is meant by "winning making us grow"?

(One small matter, of course. What *should* happen in the future doesn't automatically happen. The next time is always another ball game . . .)

So welcome to the kind of world where you have to consider what you are going to do after you win the game. There have been times in history and places on this planet when and where the question never would have come up.

Er . . .

One small omission.

The standard talk on this subject, going back generations, always included the exhortation to behave with sportsmanlike conduct, to be a good winner.

The assumption here is that you are a person of integrity. It is taken for granted that, when you come out on top, you will behave like a person of integrity. And a person of integrity observes all the good sportsmanship rules toward a beaten opponent. Integrity recognizes the integrity of other persons.

To do otherwise would be to commit a no-no.

And you don't want to go around committing no-noes, do you?

About the Author

The author is especially qualified to write a book congratulating graduates since only a few short years separate "William Nesmith" (a pen name) from his own graduation experiences.

At the time of writing the author was an Environmentalist for the State of Tennessee. He holds the Master of Science degree from the University of Kentucky and a Bachelor of Science degree from Middle Tennessee State University.

He has traveled extensively in the United States and Canada and has been a silent collaborator in two published religious novels as well as other writings. He has an intimate acquaintance with the opportunities and problems of the world of the graduate.